The Beginner's Guide to Coin Collecting: Your Path to Numismatic Mastery

Introduction
- Welcome to the World of Coin Collecting
- The Allure of Numismatics
- How This Guide Will Help You

Chapter 1: Getting Started in Coin Collecting
- 1.1 What Is Coin Collecting?
  - 1.1.1 The Allure of Coin Collecting
  - 1.1.2 The Diversity of Coin Collecting

- 1.2 The Tools of the Trade
  - 1.2.1 Magnifiers and Loupes
  - 1.2.2 Coin Albums and Holders
  - 1.2.3 Reference Books and Catalogs

- 1.3 Setting Your Collecting Goals
  - 1.3.1 Defining Your Interests
  - 1.3.2 Establishing a Budget
  - 1.3.3 Creating a Collection Plan

Chapter 2: Types of Coins to Collect
- 2.1 Ancient Coins
  - 2.1.1 Roman Coins
  - 2.1.2 Greek Coins
  - 2.1.3 Byzantine Coins

- 2.2 World Coins
  - 2.2.1 Collecting by Region
  - 2.2.2 Collecting by Time Period
  - 2.2.3 Exploring Different Currencies

- 2.3 American Coins
  - 2.3.1 U.S. Coin Series
  - 2.3.2 Key Dates and Rarities
  - 2.3.3 Commemorative Coins

- 2.4 Specialized Themes
  - 2.4.1 Animal Coins
  - 2.4.2 Famous Figures
  - 2.4.3 Historical Events

- 2.5 Error Coins
  - 2.5.1 Understanding Minting Errors
  - 2.5.2 Collecting Error Coins

Chapter 3: Where to Find Coins
- 3.1 Coin Dealers and Numismatic Shows

- 3.2 Online Marketplaces and Auctions
- 3.3 Coin Clubs and Communities
- 3.4 Estate Sales and Flea Markets
- 3.5 Coin Shops and Pawnshops
- 3.6 Friends and Family

Chapter 4: Evaluating Coin Value
- 4.1 Coin Grading
  - 4.1.1 Understanding Grading Scales
  - 4.1.2 Grading Your Coins

- 4.2 Determining Coin Value
  - 4.2.1 Factors That Affect Value
  - 4.2.2 Appraisals and Valuation Tools

Chapter 5: Building and Organizing Your Collection
- 5.1 Cataloging Your Coins
  - 5.1.1 Keeping Detailed Records
  - 5.1.2 Utilizing Inventory Software

- 5.2 Displaying Your Collection
  - 5.2.1 Coin Albums and Folders
  - 5.2.2 Coin Holders and Capsules
  - 5.2.3 Framing and Shadow Boxes

Chapter 6: Coin Care and Preservation
- 6.1 Handling and Cleaning Coins
  - 6.1.1 Safe Handling Practices
  - 6.1.2 Cleaning Techniques

- 6.2 Proper Storage
  - 6.2.1 Storing Coins in a Controlled Environment
  - 6.2.2 Long-Term Storage Solutions

- 6.3 Protecting Your Investment
  - 6.3.1 Insurance for Your Collection
  - 6.3.2 Security Measures

Chapter 7: Numismatic Resources
- 7.1 Numismatic Associations and Organizations
- 7.2 Coin Shows and Exhibitions
- 7.3 Online Forums and Communities
- 7.4 Numismatic Publications and Magazines

Chapter 8: Selling and Trading Coins
- 8.1 Knowing When to Sell
- 8.2 Selling Methods and Platforms
  - 8.2.1 Auctions and Online Marketplaces
  - 8.2.2 Coin Dealers and Appraisers

- 8.3 Trading and Bartering
- 8.4 Tax Implications

Chapter 9: Advanced Topics in Numismatics
- 9.1 Investing in Coins
- 9.2 Detecting Counterfeits
- 9.3 Grading Coins Like a Pro
- 9.4 Coin Restoration and Conservation

Chapter 10: Your Journey to Numismatic Mastery
- 10.1 Ongoing Learning and Exploration
- 10.2 Connecting with Other Collectors
- 10.3 Passing Down Your Collection
- 10.4 The Endless Rewards of Numismatics

Conclusion
- Reflecting on Your Numismatic Journey
- Encouragement for Future Collecting

Appendices
- A. Glossary of Numismatic Terms
- B. Recommended Reading and Resources
- C. Coin Grading Standards
- D. Coin Shows and Events Calendar

Index

This comprehensive outline covers the essential topics and subtopics that will guide beginners through the fascinating world of coin collecting. Whether you're interested in ancient coins, modern currency, or specialized themes, this guide will help you embark on your path to numismatic mastery.

- Welcome to the World of Coin Collecting

Welcome, aspiring numismatist, to the captivating world of coin collecting! This journey you're about to embark upon promises a wealth of historical discovery, artistic appreciation, and personal fulfillment. In the pages that follow, you'll gain invaluable insights, tips, and knowledge that will serve as your compass in navigating the rich and diverse realm of numismatics.

Coin collecting is a hobby like no other. It allows you to hold in your hands tangible pieces of history, each with its own unique tale to tell. Whether you're drawn to the intricate designs of ancient coins, the cultural diversity of world currencies, the historical significance of American coins, or the thematic exploration of specialized collections, this guide will equip you with the tools and wisdom you need to embark on your own numismatic adventure.

As you delve into the pages of "The Beginner's Guide to Coin Collecting: Your Path to Numismatic Mastery," you'll discover the fundamentals of this rewarding pursuit, learn how to select coins that resonate with your interests, and acquire the skills necessary to evaluate and care for your treasures. Whether you're a history buff, an art enthusiast, or simply looking for a hobby that offers both personal enrichment and the potential for financial gain, coin collecting has something to offer you.

So, without further ado, let's embark on this exciting journey together. By the end of this guide, you'll not only be well-versed in the art and science of coin collecting but also well on your way to becoming a seasoned numismatist. Let the adventure begin!

- The Allure of Numismatics

Numismatics, the study and collection of coins, holds an irresistible allure for enthusiasts around the world. It is a captivating hobby that transcends time and place, offering a multifaceted appeal that has intrigued individuals for centuries. The allure of numismatics can be understood through several compelling facets:

1. A Glimpse into History: Numismatics provides a tangible connection to the past. Each coin represents a distinct moment in history, carrying the imprints of the era in which it was minted. Whether it's an ancient coin from a bygone civilization or a coin from a recent historical event, collecting coins allows us to touch, feel, and study the remnants of past ages.

2. Artistry and Aesthetics: Coins are miniature works of art. The intricate designs, masterful engravings, and attention to detail exhibited on coins make them a source of visual delight. The fusion of art and history on a small metallic canvas is a captivating aspect of numismatics.

3. Cultural Exploration: Coin collecting transcends borders and cultures. It invites collectors to explore the rich diversity of the world's societies and their monetary systems. Through coins, collectors can gain insights into the customs, traditions, and values of different civilizations.

4. Educational Value: Engaging in numismatics is akin to embarking on a continuous learning journey. Collectors delve into various historical periods, political landscapes, and economic contexts. This pursuit of knowledge is intellectually stimulating and can deepen one's understanding of history and economics.

5. Personal Connection: For many collectors, numismatics holds a personal connection. Coins may serve as family heirlooms or mementos from travels, carrying sentimental value and memories of cherished moments. They become a means of preserving personal history.

6. Investment Potential: While the primary motivation for many collectors is the joy of discovery and learning, there is also the potential for financial gain. Rare and valuable coins can appreciate over time, making coin collecting an intriguing investment avenue.

7. Community and Camaraderie: Numismatics fosters a sense of community among collectors. Coin clubs, conventions, and online forums provide opportunities for enthusiasts to connect, share knowledge, and trade coins. The camaraderie among collectors adds to the social appeal of the hobby.

8. Quest for Rarity: The thrill of the hunt for rare and elusive coins is a driving force for many collectors. Discovering a coin that few others possess is a gratifying and exhilarating experience.

9. Preservation of Heritage: Numismatics plays a crucial role in preserving cultural heritage. Collectors contribute to the conservation and study of coins, ensuring that these artifacts continue to serve as windows into the past for future generations.

The allure of numismatics lies in its ability to offer a profound connection to history, a deep appreciation for artistry, and a sense of wonderment about the diversity of human civilization. As you journey deeper into the world of coin collecting, you'll uncover these facets and more, embarking on a captivating exploration that can span a lifetime.

- How This Guide Will Help You

Embarking on your journey into the world of coin collecting is an exciting and enriching endeavor. However, the path to becoming a proficient numismatist can be complex and challenging, especially for beginners. That's where this guide comes to your aid. Here's how this comprehensive resource will assist you on your numismatic journey:

1. Comprehensive Learning: This guide provides a structured and comprehensive approach to coin collecting. You'll start with the basics and gradually delve into more advanced topics, ensuring that you have a solid foundation before exploring the intricacies of numismatics.

2. Clear and Concise Explanations: Complex concepts and terminology are demystified with clear and easy-to-understand explanations. Whether you're a complete novice or someone with some prior knowledge, you'll find the content approachable and informative.

3. Guided Progression: Each chapter builds upon the knowledge gained in previous chapters. You'll follow a logical progression that takes you from understanding the fundamentals of coin collecting to mastering advanced techniques and topics.

4. Practical Tips and Strategies: Throughout the guide, you'll find practical tips and strategies to enhance your collecting experience. From selecting coins wisely to preserving and displaying your collection, you'll gain valuable insights and advice.

5. Visual Aids: Visual aids, such as images of coins and illustrations, accompany key concepts, helping you better understand grading, identifying errors, and appreciating the artistry of coins.

6. References and Resources: You'll discover a wealth of recommended reading materials, websites, and resources to further your knowledge and stay up-to-date in the ever-evolving world of numismatics.

7. Real-World Examples: Real-world examples and case studies provide context and illustrate important principles. These examples help you apply what you've learned to your own collecting endeavors.

8. Interactive Exercises: Some chapters include interactive exercises and checklists to reinforce your learning and guide you in practical aspects of coin collecting.

9. Expert Insights: Throughout the guide, you'll benefit from insights and advice from experienced collectors and numismatic experts. Their perspectives will enrich your understanding and inspire your collecting journey.

10. Inspiration and Encouragement: Coin collecting is not just a hobby; it's a passion. This guide aims to inspire and encourage you to fully immerse yourself in the world of numismatics, fostering a lifelong love for collecting coins.

Whether you're interested in building a collection for historical knowledge, artistic appreciation, personal enjoyment, or even as an investment, this guide equips you with the knowledge and tools you need to excel in the world of coin collecting. So, as you turn the pages and embark on this numismatic adventure, rest assured that you're on a path to numismatic mastery, guided by a resource designed to enhance your collecting experience at every step.

Chapter 1: Getting Started in Coin Collecting

Introduction

Welcome to the thrilling world of coin collecting, where history, artistry, and discovery converge to create a hobby like no other. This chapter marks the beginning of your numismatic journey, as we delve into the fundamental aspects of coin collecting that will set the stage for your path to numismatic mastery.

Coin collecting, often referred to as numismatics, has a rich and storied history that spans millennia. From ancient civilizations to modern nations, coins have played a pivotal role in commerce, culture, and the preservation of historical narratives. As a coin collector, you are about to embark on a quest that will transport you through time and across the globe, allowing you to hold in your hands the tangible remnants of countless human stories.

In this chapter, we will lay the groundwork for your numismatic adventure by exploring the following key areas:

1. What Is Coin Collecting?: Before diving into the details, it's essential to understand the essence of coin collecting. We'll explore the reasons people are drawn to this hobby and the diverse interests it encompasses.

2. The Tools of the Trade: Just as an artist relies on brushes and paints, a coin collector requires specific tools to pursue their passion effectively. We'll introduce you to the essential tools and supplies that will aid you in your collecting endeavors.

3. Setting Your Collecting Goals: Every collector's journey is unique. To embark on your path to numismatic mastery, you'll need to define your collecting goals, establish a budget, and create a plan that aligns with your interests and aspirations.

By the end of this chapter, you'll have a solid understanding of the basics of coin collecting and the tools needed to begin your own collection. Whether you're an absolute beginner or someone looking to refine their collecting strategy, this chapter will serve as your compass, guiding you toward a rewarding and enriching experience in the world of coin collecting. So, let's begin our exploration of this captivating hobby and set the stage for your numismatic adventure!

1.1 What Is Coin Collecting?

Coin collecting, also known as numismatics, is a captivating and multifaceted hobby centered around the acquisition, study, and appreciation of coins. Numismatists, individuals who engage in coin collecting, embark on a journey that transcends the mere accumulation of metallic currency. It is a hobby that delves deep into history, culture, artistry, and the fascinating world of currency.

At its core, coin collecting involves:

1.1.1 The Allure of Coin Collecting

The fascination with coin collecting can be attributed to a range of compelling factors:

- Historical Connection: Coins are tangible links to the past, representing different periods, civilizations, and historical events. They offer a glimpse into the economic, political, and cultural aspects of societies throughout time.

- Artistic Appreciation: Coins are miniature canvases that feature intricate designs, symbols, and engravings. Collectors often admire the artistry and craftsmanship that go into the creation of these tiny masterpieces.

- Educational Value: Numismatics is an ongoing learning experience. Collectors continuously expand their knowledge about different time periods, regions, and monetary systems as they explore their collections.

- Personal Connection: For many, coin collecting is a deeply personal endeavor. Coins can hold sentimental value, serving as reminders of travels, family legacies, or special occasions.

- Investment Potential: While some collectors focus primarily on the historical and cultural aspects of coins, others recognize the investment potential in collecting rare and valuable pieces.

- Community and Camaraderie: Coin collectors often join clubs, attend conventions, and participate in online forums, fostering connections with like-minded enthusiasts and sharing their passion for numismatics.

1.1.2 The Diversity of Coin Collecting

One of the most appealing aspects of coin collecting is its diversity. Collectors have the freedom to shape their collections according to their interests and preferences. Some common areas of specialization within coin collecting include:

- Ancient Coins: Collectors of ancient coins explore the currencies of bygone civilizations, such as Roman, Greek, and Byzantine coins. These coins provide a unique window into the past.

- World Coins: Enthusiasts of world coins amass a global collection, seeking coins from various countries and regions. This approach allows for an exploration of diverse cultures and histories.

- American Coins: American coin collectors concentrate on U.S. currency, which boasts a rich history of design changes, minting errors, and rare pieces that attract avid enthusiasts.

- Specialized Themes: Some collectors focus on specific themes, such as coins featuring animals, famous figures, or historical events. These thematic collections can be both enjoyable and educational.

- Error Coins: Collectors of error coins seek out coins with minting mistakes, ranging from minor imperfections to major errors. These coins are prized for their uniqueness.

As you embark on your own coin collecting journey, you'll have the opportunity to define your collecting goals and tailor your collection to your interests. Whether you're drawn to the mysteries of ancient civilizations, the beauty of coin designs, or the thrill of hunting for rare pieces, coin collecting offers a rich and rewarding experience. This guide will serve as your companion, providing guidance and insights to help you navigate the fascinating world of numismatics.

1.2 The Tools of the Trade

Just as any craft or hobby requires the right tools, coin collecting is no exception. To embark on your numismatic journey and engage with your collection effectively, you'll need a set of essential tools and supplies. These tools are designed to assist you in various aspects of coin collecting, from examination and identification to organization and preservation. In this section, we'll introduce you to some of the fundamental tools of the trade that will become your companions in your pursuit of numismatic knowledge and mastery.

1.2.1 Magnifiers and Loupes

One of the most fundamental tools for a coin collector is a magnifier or loupe. These devices provide close-up views of coins, allowing you to examine minute details, such as mint marks, engraving intricacies, and the overall condition of the coin. Here are a few key considerations:

- Magnification Power: Choose a magnifier or loupe with an appropriate level of magnification for your needs. Common magnification levels range from 5x to 20x, with higher magnification offering more detailed views.

- Lighting: Opt for a magnifier with built-in LED lighting or ensure you have adequate lighting in your workspace. Proper lighting is essential for accurate coin inspection.

- Quality Optics: Invest in a quality magnifier with clear optics to avoid distortion and ensure precise examination.

1.2.2 Coin Albums and Holders

Coin albums and holders are essential for organizing and protecting your coin collection. They come in various forms, each designed to accommodate different coin sizes and types. Consider the following:

- Coin Folders: These cardboard or paper folders have labeled slots for specific coin types or series. They are an economical option for organizing your coins and are often used for U.S. coin collections.

- Coin Albums: Coin albums are typically binders with plastic sleeves or pages that allow you to insert and display your coins. They come in various sizes and are suitable for world coin collections or more extensive sets.

- Coin Holders and Capsules: Individual coin holders, often made of clear plastic, protect coins from physical damage and environmental factors. Coin capsules, which are two-part plastic cases that snap together, provide additional protection and visibility.

1.2.3 Reference Books and Catalogs

A well-rounded coin collector needs access to reference books and catalogs that provide valuable information about coins. These resources assist in coin identification, valuation, and historical context. Here are some considerations:

- Numismatic Reference Books: Invest in authoritative numismatic reference books that cover specific coin series, regions, or historical periods relevant to your collection.

- Catalogs: Numismatic catalogs, such as the Standard Catalog of World Coins, are comprehensive references that list coin types, mintages, and current market values for coins from around the world.

- Online Resources: Utilize reputable numismatic websites and online databases, which offer a wealth of information, including coin images, historical background, and market values.

By acquiring and using these essential tools of the trade, you'll be well-prepared to embark on your coin collecting journey with confidence. These tools will not only help you examine and appreciate your coins but also contribute to the organization and preservation of your collection, ensuring its longevity and value.

1.3 Setting Your Collecting Goals

Before you begin assembling your coin collection, it's crucial to define your collecting goals and establish a clear direction for your numismatic journey. Coin collecting offers a vast and diverse landscape, and by determining your objectives early on, you'll be better equipped to make informed decisions about what to collect, how to allocate your resources, and how to derive the most satisfaction from your pursuit. In this section, we'll explore the process of setting your collecting goals, covering key aspects to consider:

1.3.1 Defining Your Interests

The first step in setting your collecting goals is to identify your interests within the world of numismatics. Coin collecting offers an array of fascinating possibilities, from ancient coins to modern currency, and from specialized themes to specific regions. Consider the following questions to help define your interests:

- Historical Periods: Are you drawn to a particular historical era or civilization? Do you have a preference for ancient coins that tell the stories of past empires, or are you more interested in coins from a specific century or time period?

- Geographical Focus: Are you interested in world coins, American coins, or coins from a specific country or region? Does the diversity of global currencies intrigue you, or do you prefer to focus on a narrower geographic scope?

- Specialized Themes: Are there specific themes or subjects that captivate you? Examples include coins featuring animals, famous figures, military history, or commemorative events.

- Monetary Types: Do you have a preference for a particular type of coin, such as gold, silver, copper, or paper currency?

1.3.2 Establishing a Budget

Once you've defined your collecting interests, it's essential to establish a budget for your coin collecting endeavors. Collecting coins can be as affordable or as extravagant as you choose, and setting a budget helps you manage your resources effectively. Consider the following budget-related considerations:

- Initial Investment: Determine how much you're willing and able to invest in your coin collection initially. This budget can cover the acquisition of your first coins, as well as any necessary tools and references.

- Ongoing Budget: Decide on a recurring budget for adding new coins to your collection. This could be a monthly or annual allowance dedicated to acquiring coins, which helps you maintain a sustainable collecting habit.

- Allocating Funds: Consider how you'll allocate your budget among different aspects of coin collecting, such as acquiring new coins, coin supplies (holders, albums, etc.), educational materials, and attending numismatic events.

- Long-Term Perspective: Keep in mind that coin collecting is a long-term endeavor. Establish a budget that you can maintain over time and adapt as your collecting interests evolve.

1.3.3 Creating a Collection Plan

With your interests and budget in mind, it's advisable to create a collection plan that outlines your collecting goals and strategies. A well-defined plan helps you stay focused and organized as you build and expand your collection. Consider these steps when creating your collection plan:

- Identify Key Objectives: Clearly define your short-term and long-term objectives. What specific coins or series do you aim to acquire, and what is your ultimate goal in coin collecting?

- Set Milestones: Establish milestones or benchmarks that signify your progress and achievements within your collection. These milestones can be based on the number of coins, their rarity, or their historical significance.

- Research and Education: Dedicate time to research and educate yourself about the coins you intend to collect. Understand their historical context, grading standards, and market values.

- Networking and Resources: Explore numismatic communities, clubs, and online forums to connect with fellow collectors. Seek advice and guidance from experienced collectors and utilize available resources to support your journey.

- Flexibility: While having a collection plan is essential, remain flexible and open to new discoveries and opportunities. Your interests may evolve over time, leading you in unexpected but rewarding directions.

By setting clear collecting goals, establishing a budget, and creating a collection plan, you'll lay a solid foundation for your numismatic journey. These steps will help you make informed decisions, stay motivated, and derive maximum enjoyment from the world of coin collecting. Whether you're driven by historical curiosity, artistic appreciation, or a desire to connect with fellow collectors, your goals will shape the path to numismatic mastery.

Chapter 2: Types of Coins to Collect

Introduction

As you delve deeper into the fascinating world of coin collecting, you'll discover a treasure trove of numismatic possibilities awaiting your exploration. Chapter 2 is your gateway to understanding the diverse array of coins available for collection, each offering unique historical narratives, cultural insights, and artistic beauty. Whether you're intrigued by the mystique of ancient civilizations, the richness of world cultures, the historical significance of American coinage, or the thematic allure of specialized collections, this chapter will illuminate the various avenues you can traverse in your quest for numismatic mastery.

In this chapter, we'll journey together through the captivating landscape of coin collecting, exploring the following categories and their subcategories:

2.1 Ancient Coins: These are the time-worn relics of long-forgotten empires and civilizations. Ancient coin collectors delve into the coinage of ancient Greece, Rome, Byzantium, and countless other cultures that have left their indelible marks on history.

2.2 World Coins: For collectors who crave diversity, world coins offer a global adventure. You can traverse continents and centuries, amassing coins from different nations, regions, and historical epochs.

2.3 American Coins: The United States boasts a rich history of coinage, from colonial times to the modern era. American coin collectors delve into series like the Lincoln Cent, Morgan Dollar, and Buffalo Nickel, discovering the stories behind these iconic pieces.

2.4 Specialized Themes: Numismatics extends far beyond dates and denominations. Collectors with specific passions may choose to focus on themes such as animals, famous figures, or significant historical events.

2.5 Error Coins: Numismatists with a keen eye for detail seek out error coins, which carry minting mistakes that make them rare and intriguing. These coins add an element of excitement to the hobby.

By exploring these diverse categories, you'll gain insights into the breadth and depth of coin collecting, allowing you to select the path that resonates most with your interests and curiosities. Whether you aspire to build a comprehensive world coin collection, uncover the mysteries of ancient civilizations, or specialize in a particular theme, this chapter will serve as your guide, shedding light on the remarkable possibilities that await you in the world of numismatics. So, let's embark on this journey of discovery, where history, culture, and artistry converge in the form of coins, each with its own story to tell.

2.1 Ancient Coins

Ancient coins represent an enchanting realm of numismatics that beckons collectors to explore the distant echoes of history. These coins are not merely currency but rather miniature time capsules that transport collectors back to the empires, city-states, and civilizations of bygone eras. Collectors of ancient coins embark on a captivating journey into the past, where the numismatic artifacts they acquire are imbued with stories of conquests, rulers, cultural exchanges, and daily life in antiquity.

Ancient coins can be broadly categorized into several subcategories, each with its own allure:

2.1.1 Roman Coins

Roman coins are among the most renowned and collected ancient coins in the world. The Roman Empire, with its vast expanse and long history, produced an astonishing array of coinage. Collectors of Roman coins have the opportunity to delve into the diverse series minted by the Roman Republic and the Roman Empire. These coins feature the likenesses of emperors, depictions of gods and goddesses, and historical events, offering a comprehensive view of Roman culture and society.

2.1.2 Greek Coins

Greek coins provide a window into the ancient Greek world, showcasing the city-states, cultures, and artistic achievements of ancient Greece. From the iconic Athenian Owl to the powerful imagery of Alexander the Great, Greek coins are celebrated for their exquisite artistry and historical significance. Collectors of Greek coins explore the pantheon of Greek gods, mythological stories, and the fascinating evolution of coinage across various city-states.

2.1.3 Byzantine Coins

The Byzantine Empire, with its capital in Constantinople (modern-day Istanbul), produced a distinct and enduring coinage. Byzantine coins feature intricate Christian iconography, portraits of emperors, and a blend of Roman and Eastern influences. Collectors of Byzantine coins uncover the religious and political developments of the Byzantine Empire, from the early days of Constantine the Great to the final days of the empire.

Collecting ancient coins is not only a pursuit of historical knowledge but also an appreciation of artistry, craftsmanship, and the enduring legacy of ancient civilizations. These coins bear witness to the rise and fall of empires, the circulation of ideas, and the passage of time itself. As you explore the world of ancient coins, you'll become a steward of these remarkable relics, preserving the stories of the past for future generations to discover and appreciate.

2.2 World Coins

World coins encompass a vast and diverse universe of numismatic treasures that beckon collectors to embark on a global journey through history, culture, and artistry. Unlike ancient or American coins, which are often limited to specific regions or time periods, world coins offer an expansive panorama of currency from countries across the globe, spanning centuries of human civilization.

Collectors of world coins have the privilege of exploring an array of captivating themes, designs, and historical contexts. Here are some key aspects of world coin collecting:

2.2.1 Geographic Diversity

One of the most appealing aspects of world coins is the geographic diversity they offer. As a world coin collector, you can traverse continents and explore the monetary systems of different nations and regions. From the European treasures of the Renaissance to the exotic allure of Asian currencies, the world of numismatics is your passport to a global adventure.

2.2.2 Historical Variety

World coins reflect the rich tapestry of human history. Each coin carries the imprints of its era, whether it's an ancient coin from the Silk Road, a colonial coin from the New World, or a modern coin from a post-independence nation. Collectors of world coins can immerse themselves in the historical narratives, revolutions, and cultural shifts that have shaped our world.

2.2.3 Artistic Excellence

The artistry and design of world coins are a testament to the creativity and cultural expressions of different civilizations. From intricate patterns and motifs to portraits of iconic figures, world coins are miniature works of art. Collectors appreciate the diversity of artistic styles, from the classic elegance of European coinage to the vibrant symbolism of African currencies.

2.2.4 Numismatic Education

World coin collecting is not only an enriching hobby but also a continuous journey of education. Collectors learn about the history, politics, and cultural heritage of various countries. They develop an understanding of different monetary systems, coin denominations, and the significance of coin designs.

2.2.5 Themes and Specializations

Within the realm of world coins, collectors have the flexibility to focus on specific themes or regions that resonate with their interests. Whether it's collecting coins featuring animals, maritime history, famous figures, or commemorative events, world coin collectors can tailor their collections to reflect their passions.

2.2.6 Diversity of Materials

World coins are crafted from a variety of metals, including gold, silver, copper, and nickel. This diversity of materials adds an extra layer of intrigue to world coin collecting, as different metals have unique characteristics and aesthetics.

As you venture into the world of world coin collecting, you'll embark on a journey that celebrates global heritage, artistic ingenuity, and the enduring stories of nations. Each coin you acquire becomes a tangible connection to a different part of the world, offering a glimpse into the past and an appreciation of human diversity and creativity. Whether you collect coins for their historical significance, artistic beauty, or cultural appeal, world coin collecting promises a lifetime of exploration and discovery.

2.3 American Coins

American coin collecting offers a captivating exploration of the history, culture, and monetary evolution of the United States. From the earliest colonial days to the modern era, American coins tell the story of a nation's growth, its struggles, and its triumphs. Collectors of American coins delve into a vast and diverse landscape of numismatic treasures, each coin representing a unique chapter in the nation's history.

Here are some key aspects of American coin collecting:

2.3.1 Colonial Coins

The history of American coinage begins with colonial coins. These early issues, minted by the individual colonies and states before the establishment of the U.S. Mint, are highly sought after by collectors. Colonial coins offer insights into the economic and political landscape of the pre-revolutionary period.

2.3.2 U.S. Minted Coins

The United States Mint, established in 1792, has produced an extensive range of coin series and denominations over the years. Collectors of U.S. Minted Coins can explore iconic series such as:

- The Lincoln Cent: Featuring the beloved 16th President of the United States, Abraham Lincoln, and spanning numerous design changes and variations.

- The Morgan Dollar: A silver dollar coin with a storied history, associated with the Wild West and the silver mining boom.

- The Buffalo Nickel: Celebrating the spirit of the American West with its iconic buffalo and Native American design.

- The Walking Liberty Half Dollar: Known for its stunning depiction of Lady Liberty walking toward the rising sun, symbolizing freedom and progress.

2.3.3 Commemorative Coins

American coin collectors often have a keen interest in commemorative coins. These special issues mark significant events, anniversaries, and cultural milestones in American history. Commemorative coins celebrate a wide range of themes, from the bicentennial of the U.S. Constitution to the achievements of famous Americans.

2.3.4 Bullion and Precious Metals

For collectors who appreciate the intrinsic value of precious metals, American bullion coins like the American Gold Eagle and American Silver Eagle are highly regarded. These coins are not only sought after for their numismatic appeal but also as a means of investing in gold and silver.

2.3.5 Error Coins and Varieties

American coin collecting can also involve the pursuit of error coins and varieties. Numismatists often seek out coins with minting mistakes or unique die varieties that make them rare and valuable. These nuances add excitement and intrigue to collecting American coins.

2.3.6 Historical Significance

Many American coins hold deep historical significance. Whether it's the Civil War era, the Gold Rush, or the Great Depression, collecting American coins allows enthusiasts to explore pivotal moments in the nation's past.

American coin collecting is not only a means of preserving history but also a way of celebrating the enduring spirit of the United States. Each coin serves as a tangible link to the nation's heritage, offering collectors the opportunity to connect with the stories and personalities that have shaped the American experience. Whether you're drawn to the elegance of classic designs or the allure of modern bullion coins, American coin collecting promises an enriching and patriotic journey through numismatics.

2.4 Specialized Themes

Specialized theme collecting in the world of numismatics is a captivating pursuit that allows collectors to focus on specific subjects, motifs, or historical narratives within the vast realm of coin collecting. While many collectors seek coins based on regions, eras, or denominations, specialized theme collectors channel their passion into collecting coins that tell a particular story or represent a specific interest. This approach adds depth and personal meaning to a coin collection. Here are some intriguing aspects of specialized theme collecting:

2.4.1 Thematic Diversity

Specialized theme collecting covers a broad spectrum of interests, and collectors can choose from an array of captivating themes. Some popular thematic categories include:

- Animals: Collectors focus on coins featuring a variety of animals, from beloved pets to endangered species and mythical creatures.

- Famous Figures: Coins showcasing famous historical figures, leaders, and cultural icons provide a unique window into their lives and legacies.

- Historical Events: Collecting coins commemorating significant historical events, battles, or revolutions allows collectors to explore the past through numismatic lens.

- Transportation and Technology: Coins featuring modes of transportation, innovations, and technological advancements offer insights into human progress and ingenuity.

- Art and Culture: Collectors with a passion for art and culture may seek coins adorned with famous artworks, architectural landmarks, or traditional symbols.

2.4.2 Personal Connection

One of the most rewarding aspects of specialized theme collecting is the personal connection it fosters. Collectors often choose themes that resonate with their own interests, hobbies, or values. This personal connection adds a layer of passion and enthusiasm to the pursuit, making it a deeply gratifying hobby.

2.4.3 Research and Knowledge

Collecting coins based on specialized themes often requires research and knowledge about the subject matter. Whether it's delving into the history of a famous figure or studying the symbolism of a particular animal, specialized theme collectors become experts in their chosen field, expanding their understanding with each new addition to their collection.

2.4.4 Display and Presentation

Coins collected around a specific theme can be creatively displayed and presented to enhance their impact. Collectors often curate themed exhibits or displays that showcase the coins' connection to a broader narrative or story.

2.4.5 Networking and Sharing

Collectors of specialized themes often find like-minded enthusiasts who share their passion. Numismatic clubs, online forums, and exhibitions provide opportunities to connect with others who appreciate the same themes, fostering a sense of community and camaraderie.

Whether you're drawn to the majesty of wildlife, the legacy of great leaders, or the beauty of artistic expressions, specialized theme collecting allows you to channel your interests and curiosities into a numismatic adventure. Each coin you acquire becomes a piece of a larger puzzle, contributing to a collection that tells a compelling story or reflects your unique passions. Specialized theme collecting is a journey of exploration, discovery, and personal enrichment within the world of numismatics.

2.5 Error Coins

Error coins hold a special place in the hearts of numismatists and collectors, offering a thrilling and unique dimension to the world of coin collecting. These coins are not like the rest; they bear imperfections, anomalies, and irregularities that make them intriguing and highly sought after. Collectors of error coins are fascinated by the mistakes made during the minting process, which result in coins that deviate from the norm. Here are some key aspects of collecting error coins:

2.5.1 What Are Error Coins?

Error coins are coins that exhibit unintended variations from the standard production process. These variations can occur at different stages of minting and may affect various aspects of the coin, including:

- Planchet Errors: Issues related to the blank metal disc (planchet) before striking, such as off-center strikes, clipped planchets, and laminations.

- Die Errors: Mistakes occurring on the dies used to strike coins, leading to doubled dies, clashed dies, or die cracks.

- Striking Errors: Errors that take place during the coin-striking process, such as brockages (coins struck twice), multiple strikes, or incomplete strikes.

- Design Errors: Errors that affect the design or inscriptions on the coin, such as missing or misplaced mint marks, overdates, or wrong metal errors.

2.5.2 Rarity and Value

Error coins are prized for their rarity and uniqueness. Due to the unpredictable nature of minting errors, many error coins are scarce, and some are one-of-a-kind. Collectors value error coins for their novelty and historical significance, which can lead to higher market values compared to regular coins of the same type.

2.5.3 Types of Error Coins

Error coins come in a wide range of types and categories, each with its own charm:

- Double Dies: These errors occur when a coin is struck more than once with the same die, resulting in doubled images and inscriptions.

- Off-Center Strikes: Coins that were not properly centered on the dies during striking may display a portion of the design missing or cut off.

- Clipped Planchets: Planchets with missing or partially missing sections due to improper punching during the blanking process.

- Cuds: Coins with raised, blob-like features on the surface caused by die cracks.

- Mint Mark Errors: Errors involving the placement, size, or shape of mint marks, which identify the coin's minting location.

2.5.4 The Thrill of Discovery

Collecting error coins offers a sense of adventure and discovery. Finding an error coin in circulation or within a collection can be an exhilarating experience for numismatists. The search for these hidden treasures adds an element of excitement to the hobby.

2.5.5 The Challenges of Authentication

Authenticating error coins can be a complex process. Collectors often rely on experts or grading services to verify the legitimacy of a particular error and assess its grade. Authentication is crucial, as some counterfeit coins attempt to mimic error characteristics.

2.5.6 Variations and Subvarieties

Error coins can have multiple variations and subvarieties based on the nature and extent of the error. Collectors often delve into the nuances of different error types within a series, expanding their knowledge and collections.

Collecting error coins is an adventure filled with surprises and the potential for remarkable discoveries. These coins represent a fascinating intersection of history and human error, offering collectors a unique perspective on the minting process and the artistry of coinage. Whether you're drawn to dramatic double dies or subtle planchet errors, error coin collecting is a pursuit that promises continual intrigue and the possibility of uncovering numismatic treasures.

Chapter 3: Where to Find Coins

Introduction

Having embarked on your numismatic journey and gained insights into the captivating world of coin collecting, you're now ready to take the next step: acquiring the coins that will form the heart of your collection. Chapter 3 serves as your guide to the diverse avenues and sources where you can find coins to add to your growing collection.

From the thrill of uncovering hidden treasures in your pocket change to the excitement of attending coin shows and auctions, this chapter explores the myriad ways in which collectors acquire coins. We'll also delve into the world of coin dealers, online marketplaces, and the art of coin trading. Whether you're seeking ancient coins with historical significance, world coins that transport you to distant lands, or American coins that tell the story of a nation, this chapter will equip you with the knowledge and strategies to locate the coins that resonate with your collecting goals.

As you venture into the realm of coin acquisition, keep in mind that each coin you add to your collection is not merely an object of value; it's a tangible piece of history, a work of art, and a source of pride for any collector. So, let's explore the diverse avenues available to you, and embark on a treasure hunt through the numismatic world, where every coin tells a story and every acquisition becomes a cherished addition to your collection.

3.1 Coin Dealers and Numismatic Shows

Coin dealers and numismatic shows are foundational pillars of the coin collecting community, offering collectors valuable opportunities to acquire coins, expand their knowledge, and connect with fellow enthusiasts. In this section, we will explore the world of coin dealers and numismatic shows as essential sources for finding coins to enhance your collection.

3.1.1 Coin Dealers

Coin dealers play a central role in the numismatic ecosystem. These professionals are experts in coins and currency, and they specialize in buying, selling, and appraising coins. Coin dealers can be found in various forms, including:

- Brick-and-Mortar Coin Shops: Physical storefronts where collectors can browse, buy, and sell coins. These shops often carry a diverse inventory and provide an opportunity for in-person consultations.

- Online Coin Dealers: Many coin dealers operate e-commerce websites, making it convenient for collectors to browse and purchase coins from the comfort of their homes. Reputable online dealers offer detailed coin descriptions, high-quality images, and secure transactions.

- Coin Shows and Conventions: Dealers frequently participate in coin shows and conventions, where they showcase their coin offerings and engage with collectors. These events provide a unique opportunity for face-to-face interactions and the chance to examine coins in person.

When dealing with coin dealers, consider the following tips:

- Research and Reputation: Look for dealers with a solid reputation within the numismatic community.

Read reviews, seek recommendations, and verify their credentials.

- Knowledge and Expertise: Choose dealers who specialize in the types of coins you collect. Their expertise can be invaluable in assisting you with acquisitions and appraisals.

- Fair Pricing: Compare prices and ensure that you receive fair value for your purchases or sales. It's essential to have a clear understanding of the market value of the coins you're interested in.

- Authentication and Certification: Inquire about the authenticity and certification of coins. Reputable dealers often sell coins that have been professionally graded and encapsulated by third-party grading services.

3.1.2 Numismatic Shows and Conventions

Numismatic shows and conventions are vibrant gatherings of coin collectors, dealers, and enthusiasts. These events provide a dynamic environment where collectors can explore a wide array of coins, discover rare pieces, and immerse themselves in the numismatic community. Key features of numismatic shows include:

- Diverse Inventory: Shows feature a diverse selection of coins, ranging from ancient and world coins to American issues and specialized themes. Collectors can find coins that align with their interests and objectives.

- Networking: Numismatic shows offer a unique opportunity to network with fellow collectors, experts, and dealers. You can share insights, exchange knowledge, and foster connections within the coin collecting community.

- Educational Programs: Many shows host educational programs, seminars, and presentations on various numismatic topics. These sessions enhance your understanding of coins, grading, and the historical context of numismatics.

- Auctions: Some numismatic shows include coin auctions, where collectors can bid on coins of interest. Auctions provide an exciting platform to acquire rare and valuable coins.

- Exhibits: Coin exhibits at shows showcase exceptional collections, providing inspiration and insights for collectors. You can gain a deeper appreciation for the artistry and history of coins through these exhibits.

To make the most of numismatic shows:

- Plan Ahead: Research upcoming shows and conventions, noting their locations, dates, and featured dealers. Plan your visit accordingly.

- Bring a List: Come prepared with a list of the coins you're seeking or the areas of numismatics you want to explore. This will help you stay focused during the event.

- Attend Seminars: Take advantage of educational opportunities by attending seminars and presentations. You'll expand your knowledge and meet like-minded collectors.

- Engage with Dealers: Interact with dealers to discuss your collecting goals and explore their offerings. Building relationships with dealers can lead to exciting coin discoveries.

Coin dealers and numismatic shows are integral parts of the coin collecting experience. They offer access to a wide range of coins, valuable insights, and connections within the numismatic community. Whether you're a seasoned collector or just beginning your journey, these resources provide essential avenues for acquiring coins and enriching your collecting experience.

3.2 Online Marketplaces and Auctions

In the digital age, coin collectors have unprecedented access to a global marketplace of coins through online platforms and auctions. This section explores the world of online coin marketplaces and auctions as powerful tools for finding and acquiring coins for your collection.

3.2.1 Online Coin Marketplaces

Online coin marketplaces are virtual venues where collectors can browse, buy, and sell coins. These platforms offer a vast and diverse inventory of coins from around the world, making it convenient for collectors to explore and acquire pieces that align with their interests. Key features of online coin marketplaces include:

- Diverse Selection: Online marketplaces host a wide variety of coins, from ancient and world issues to American denominations and specialized themes. Collectors can easily search for coins that match their preferences.

- Convenience: Online platforms allow collectors to browse and shop from the comfort of their homes, providing 24/7 access to coin listings.

- Detailed Listings: Listings on reputable online marketplaces typically include high-resolution images, detailed descriptions, and pricing information. Collectors can make informed decisions based on these listings.

- Seller Ratings: Many online marketplaces incorporate seller ratings and reviews, enabling buyers to assess the reputation and reliability of sellers before making purchases.

- Secure Transactions: Reputable online marketplaces prioritize secure transactions, protecting both buyers and sellers through secure payment systems and buyer protection programs.

When using online coin marketplaces:

- Research Sellers: Prioritize sellers with positive ratings and reviews. Establishing a good rapport with trusted sellers can lead to successful and satisfying transactions.

- Verify Authenticity: Be cautious and verify the authenticity of coins, especially when dealing with rare or valuable pieces. Look for sellers who provide certification or authentication information.

- Compare Prices: Take advantage of the wide selection to compare prices and find the best deals. Consider factors such as coin condition, rarity, and market demand when assessing pricing.

3.2.2 Online Coin Auctions

Online coin auctions are exciting platforms for collectors seeking rare and valuable coins. These auctions feature a diverse array of coins, from unique numismatic treasures to highly sought-after pieces. Key aspects of online coin auctions include:

- Bidding: Collectors can participate in auctions by placing bids on coins of interest. Auction formats may include traditional timed auctions or dynamic auctions with live bidding.

- Competition: Auctions often attract competitive bidding, which can drive up prices for desirable coins. Collectors should set a budget and bid strategically to secure their desired acquisitions.

- Auction Houses: Reputable auction houses host online coin auctions, providing a trustworthy platform for buying and selling coins. These houses typically offer detailed catalog listings and expert descriptions.

- Proxy Bidding: Many online auctions use proxy bidding, where participants set their maximum bid, and the system automatically increases their bid incrementally to maintain their position as the highest bidder, up to their maximum amount.

- Authentication and Certification: Auction houses often provide authentication and grading information for coins in their auctions. This transparency adds credibility to the listings.

To make the most of online coin auctions:

- Research Catalogs: Explore auction catalogs well in advance to identify coins of interest. Carefully read descriptions and assess coin condition from provided images.

- Set a Budget: Establish a budget for each coin you wish to bid on and stick to it. Auctions can be competitive, and it's easy to get caught up in the excitement of bidding.

- Bid Strategically: Place bids strategically, considering the coin's estimated value, market demand, and your own collecting goals. Avoid overbidding to stay within your budget.

- Monitor Auctions: Keep a close eye on auctions as they approach their closing times. Be prepared to adjust your bids if necessary.

Online marketplaces and auctions offer collectors unparalleled access to a vast array of coins, providing opportunities to acquire rare and coveted pieces. These platforms combine the convenience of online shopping with the thrill of competitive bidding, making them valuable resources for collectors at all levels of experience. Whether you're seeking a specific coin to complete your collection or aiming to uncover hidden gems, online marketplaces and auctions offer exciting possibilities for enhancing your numismatic journey.

3.3 Coin Clubs and Communities

Coin clubs and numismatic communities are vibrant hubs of interaction, education, and collaboration for coin collectors. Joining these groups can significantly enrich your collecting experience and provide valuable opportunities to find coins, learn from others, and share your passion. In this section, we explore the role of coin clubs and communities as essential sources for acquiring coins and expanding your numismatic knowledge.

3.3.1 Coin Clubs

Coin clubs are local or regional organizations comprised of individuals who share a common interest in coin collecting. These clubs typically meet regularly, fostering camaraderie among members and providing a platform for educational activities, coin exchanges, and group projects. Key features of coin clubs include:

- Local Connection: Coin clubs offer a chance to connect with fellow collectors in your community or region. Meeting in person allows for face-to-face interactions and the opportunity to build lasting friendships.

- Educational Opportunities: Clubs often host presentations, lectures, and discussions on various numismatic topics. These educational activities enhance your understanding of coins and their historical context.

- Coin Exchanges: Many coin clubs organize coin exchanges or trading sessions during meetings, where members can buy, sell, or trade coins with one another. These exchanges are an excellent way to find new additions for your collection.

- Group Projects: Some clubs engage in group projects, such as coin exhibits, coin displays at local events, or collaborative research efforts. Participating in these projects can be rewarding and intellectually stimulating.

- Access to Resources: Clubs often have access to resources such as numismatic libraries, reference materials, and specialized knowledge. These resources can aid your research and collecting endeavors.

To benefit fully from coin clubs:

- Join Locally: Seek out coin clubs in your area and consider joining one that aligns with your collecting interests. Attending meetings and participating in club activities can be both enjoyable and informative.

- Engage Actively: Actively participate in club meetings and events. Share your knowledge and experiences with fellow members and take advantage of the expertise within the club.

3.3.2 Online Numismatic Communities

Online numismatic communities, including forums, social media groups, and websites, have become essential sources of information, engagement, and coin acquisitions in the digital age. These communities offer a global platform for collectors to connect, share their collections, seek advice, and discover coins. Key aspects of online numismatic communities include:

- Global Reach: Online communities bring together collectors from around the world, offering diverse perspectives and a wealth of numismatic knowledge.

- Discussion Forums: Numismatic forums enable members to engage in discussions, seek advice, and share their coin acquisitions. Popular forums cover a wide range of topics and themes.

- Online Marketplaces: Some online communities have integrated marketplaces where members can buy, sell, or trade coins. These marketplaces often include a diverse selection of coins from various collectors.

- Collecting Journals and Blogs: Many collectors maintain online journals or blogs where they document their collecting journey, share insights, and showcase their coin acquisitions.

- Social Media Groups: Platforms like Facebook, Reddit, and Instagram host numismatic groups and pages where collectors can connect and share their collections.

To make the most of online numismatic communities:

- Participate Actively: Engage in discussions, share your collecting experiences, and seek advice from fellow members. Actively participating in online communities can help you build connections and learn from others.

- Follow Trusted Sources: Be cautious when buying coins from online sources and verify the credibility of sellers. Consider purchasing from well-established members with positive feedback and reviews.

Coin clubs and online numismatic communities provide collectors with opportunities for learning, networking, and coin acquisitions. By actively engaging with these groups, you can expand your knowledge, discover new coins, and connect with fellow enthusiasts who share your passion for numismatics. Whether you prefer the local camaraderie of a coin club or the global reach of online communities, these resources are invaluable for collectors seeking to enhance their numismatic experience.

3.4 Estate Sales and Flea Markets

Estate sales and flea markets are treasure troves for coin collectors on the hunt for unique and unexpected finds. These venues offer the excitement of discovering coins amidst a wide array of items, making them excellent sources for uncovering hidden numismatic gems. In this section, we explore the world of estate sales and flea markets as unconventional yet rewarding places to acquire coins.

3.4.1 Estate Sales

Estate sales are typically held to liquidate the belongings of a deceased person or to downsize an individual's possessions. These sales often feature a wide range of items, including furniture, antiques, collectibles, and, importantly for coin collectors, coins and currency. Here are key aspects of estate sales as a source for acquiring coins:

- Varied Inventory: Estate sales offer a diverse inventory of items, and coins may be found among the belongings. Coins may be stored in coin albums, jars, boxes, or safes, waiting to be discovered by astute collectors.

- Surprise Finds: Estate sales can yield surprise finds, including rare coins, vintage banknotes, and unique collections. Many collectors have stories of uncovering valuable coins at estate sales.

- Bargaining Opportunities: Estate sales often allow for negotiations on prices, giving collectors the chance to acquire coins at favorable rates. Bargaining with estate sale organizers or estate representatives can be part of the experience.

To make the most of estate sales:

- Research and Plan: Keep an eye on estate sale listings in your area, both online and in local newspapers. Plan your visits based on sales that advertise coins or collectibles.

- Inspect Thoroughly: When attending an estate sale, examine items carefully. Coins may be tucked away in unexpected places, so take your time to search for hidden treasures.

- Bring Cash: Estate sales typically prefer cash payments, so be prepared with sufficient funds if you intend to make purchases.

3.4.2 Flea Markets

Flea markets are bustling marketplaces where vendors sell a wide assortment of goods, including vintage items, antiques, collectibles, and, importantly for coin collectors, coins and currency. Flea markets can be both physical and online, offering collectors opportunities to browse, negotiate, and acquire coins. Key features of flea markets as a source for acquiring coins include:

- Vendor Variety: Flea markets attract a diverse group of vendors, each with their own assortment of items. Collectors can encounter dealers specializing in coins, currency, or numismatic collectibles.

- Negotiation: Flea market purchases often involve negotiations on prices, allowing collectors to secure coins at competitive rates. Haggling is a common practice, so be prepared to engage in friendly bargaining.

- Assorted Inventory: Flea market vendors may have coins from various regions, time periods, and denominations. This variety can lead to unexpected discoveries.

To make the most of flea markets:

- Plan Ahead: Research local flea markets or explore online flea market platforms to identify potential sources for coins. Plan your visit or browsing session accordingly.

- Ask Questions: Engage with vendors to inquire about their coin offerings, ask questions about the coins' history or provenance, and negotiate prices when appropriate.

- Inspect Coins: When examining coins at flea markets, assess their condition, authenticity, and any visible signs of wear. Knowledge of coin grading can be beneficial.

Estate sales and flea markets provide collectors with the thrill of discovery and the opportunity to acquire coins in unconventional settings. These venues may yield unique numismatic treasures that add excitement and diversity to your collection. Whether you stumble upon a hidden coin collection at an estate sale or negotiate a favorable deal at a flea market, these untraditional sources can lead to rewarding numismatic experiences.

3.5 Coin Shops and Pawnshops

Coin shops and pawnshops are traditional brick-and-mortar establishments that cater to coin collectors and enthusiasts alike. These physical locations provide collectors with the opportunity to browse, purchase, and sometimes sell coins in a dedicated numismatic setting. In this section, we explore the role of coin shops and pawnshops as valuable sources for acquiring coins.

3.5.1 Coin Shops

Coin shops, also known as coin stores or numismatic shops, are specialty stores that primarily focus on coins, currency, and related collectibles. These establishments are staffed by knowledgeable experts who can assist collectors in finding the right coins for their collections. Key aspects of coin shops as a source for acquiring coins include:

- Specialized Inventory: Coin shops specialize in coins from various regions, historical periods, and denominations. They often carry a wide selection of numismatic items, catering to collectors with diverse interests.

- Expert Guidance: The staff at coin shops are typically well-versed in numismatics and can provide expert guidance on coin selection, valuation, and grading. Collectors can benefit from the expertise of these professionals.

- Examination and Authentication: Coin shops allow collectors to physically examine and authenticate coins before making a purchase. This hands-on experience ensures that collectors are satisfied with their acquisitions.

- Local Presence: Coin shops have a physical presence in local communities, making them accessible to collectors who prefer in-person interactions. Visiting a coin shop can be an educational and social experience.

To make the most of coin shops:

- Visit Locally: Locate coin shops in your area and plan visits to explore their inventory. Engaging with knowledgeable staff can enhance your collecting journey.

- Build Relationships: Establish relationships with the staff and owners of coin shops. Building trust with reputable dealers can lead to opportunities to acquire valuable coins.

3.5.2 Pawnshops

Pawnshops are businesses that offer loans in exchange for personal property, including coins and collectibles. These establishments can also sell items that have been forfeited or pawned by individuals. While pawnshops may not specialize in numismatics to the same extent as coin shops, they can still serve as sources for acquiring coins. Key aspects of pawnshops as a source for acquiring coins include:

- Varied Inventory: Pawnshops may have a diverse range of items, including coins and currency. Collectors may encounter coins from various regions and time periods.

- Negotiation: Purchasing coins from pawnshops often involves negotiations on prices. Collectors can explore the possibility of acquiring coins at competitive rates.

- Unexpected Finds: Pawnshops can yield unexpected finds, including rare or valuable coins that may have been pawned by individuals who were unaware of their numismatic worth.

To make the most of pawnshops:

- Research Ahead: Research pawnshops in your area or explore online listings to identify potential sources for coins. Be prepared to visit the shops or contact them to inquire about coin offerings.

- Inspect Coins: When examining coins at pawnshops, assess their condition, authenticity, and any visible signs of wear. Knowledge of coin grading can be helpful in making informed decisions.

Coin shops and pawnshops offer collectors opportunities to acquire coins in a physical retail setting. Whether you're seeking expert guidance and a wide selection at a coin shop or exploring the inventory of a pawnshop for hidden numismatic treasures, these traditional sources can add depth and variety to your coin collection.

3.6 Friends and Family

While coin collecting often involves searching far and wide for unique pieces, sometimes, valuable additions to your collection can be found much closer to home. Friends and family members can unknowingly possess coins that hold sentimental or historical significance. In this section, we explore the role of friends and family as unexpected sources for acquiring coins.

3.6.1 Inherited Collections

In many cases, individuals inherit coin collections from family members, such as grandparents, parents, or other relatives. These inherited collections can be a source of valuable coins and personal connections to numismatic history. Key aspects of inherited collections include:

- Sentimental Value: Coins passed down through generations often hold sentimental value, as they may be associated with cherished family memories or stories.

- Historical Significance: Inherited collections can include coins that were in circulation during specific historical events or eras, providing a tangible link to the past.

- Hidden Treasures: Family members may not always be aware of the full value or significance of the coins they possess. Collectors can uncover hidden treasures within inherited collections.

To make the most of inherited collections:

- Ask and Inquire: Approach family members and inquire about any coins or collectibles that may have been passed down. Understanding the history and context of the collection can provide insights into its significance.

- Preservation: Ensure that inherited coins are properly preserved and stored to maintain their condition and value. Consider professional grading or appraisal if necessary.

3.6.2 Personal Connections

Friends and acquaintances may also have coins in their possession, whether as part of their own collections or as items they have come across over the years. These personal connections can sometimes lead to opportunities to acquire coins. Key aspects of personal connections as a source for acquiring coins include:

- Informal Transactions: Friends or acquaintances may be open to informal transactions involving coins. They may be willing to sell, trade, or gift coins that align with your interests.

- Shared Interests: Coin collectors often connect with others who share their passion. Building friendships with fellow collectors can lead to coin-related exchanges and discoveries.

- Collecting Stories: Engaging in conversations with friends and acquaintances about your interest in coin collecting can lead to discussions about their own experiences or collections.

To make the most of personal connections:

- Share Your Interest: Let your friends and acquaintances know about your interest in coin collecting. You may discover shared interests or receive offers related to coins.

- Respect Boundaries: Approach coin-related discussions with sensitivity and respect. Not everyone may be interested in parting with their coins, so it's important to be considerate of their preferences.

Acquiring coins through friends and family connections can offer a unique dimension to your collection. These coins may come with personal stories and memories, making them even more meaningful to collectors. By fostering open and respectful discussions with loved ones and acquaintances, you may uncover coins that hold both sentimental and numismatic value, adding depth to your collection and strengthening your connections with those around you.

Chapter 4: Evaluating Coin Value

Introduction

As a budding numismatist, you've embarked on a captivating journey through the world of coin collecting, exploring the rich tapestry of history, culture, and artistry that coins embody. Now, in Chapter 4, we delve into the essential aspect of numismatics: evaluating the value of coins. Understanding the worth of your coin collection is not only a practical endeavor but also a thrilling part of the hobby.

In this chapter, we will unravel the intricate facets of coin valuation, equipping you with the knowledge and skills needed to assess the monetary and historical significance of your coins. Whether you're curious about the value of a cherished family heirloom, evaluating a recent acquisition, or simply interested in gauging the worth of your collection, this chapter will guide you through the process.

We will explore the various factors that influence a coin's value, from its rarity and condition to its historical context and demand among collectors. Additionally, you'll learn about the importance of coin grading, authentication, and market trends in determining value. Armed with this understanding, you'll be well-prepared to navigate the world of coin appraisal, sales, and acquisitions with confidence.

Remember that while evaluating the monetary value of your coins is a crucial aspect of numismatics, the true worth of your collection extends far beyond the numbers. Each coin is a window into history, a piece of art, and a source of fascination. So, let's embark on this numismatic journey and uncover the secrets to evaluating the value of your coin collection, enriching your appreciation for the world of numismatics along the way.

4.1 Coin Grading

Coin grading is a fundamental aspect of evaluating the value and condition of coins. Grading provides a standardized way to assess the physical state of a coin, allowing collectors, dealers, and investors to make informed decisions about buying, selling, and collecting coins. In this section, we will explore the importance of coin grading and the key elements involved in the grading process.

4.1.1 Why Coin Grading Matters

Coin grading serves several crucial purposes in numismatics:

1. Determining Value: Grading provides a basis for assigning a coin's market value. Coins in higher grades are generally more valuable than those in lower grades, all other factors being equal.

2. Authenticity Verification: Grading helps verify the authenticity of a coin. Third-party grading services use expertise and technology to identify counterfeit or altered coins.

3. Standardization: Grading sets a standardized scale for describing a coin's condition. This common language facilitates accurate communication among collectors, dealers, and experts.

4. Preservation: Grading helps collectors and institutions make informed decisions about the preservation and conservation of coins.

4.1.2 The Grading Scale

The most widely used grading scale for coins is the Sheldon Coin Grading Scale, which assigns a numerical grade to a coin based on its condition. The scale ranges from 1 to 70, with each number representing a specific grade. The key grades include:

- Poor (PO-1) to Fair (FR-2): Coins in these grades are heavily worn and often barely recognizable.

- Good (G-4) to Very Fine (VF-20): Coins in this range show varying degrees of wear, with Good being the lowest and Very Fine displaying moderate wear.

- Extremely Fine (EF-40) to About Uncirculated (AU-58): Coins in this range have minimal wear and exhibit sharp details. About Uncirculated coins show nearly full luster.

- Mint State (MS-60 to MS-70): These coins are uncirculated and have no wear. Mint State coins are further divided into subgrades, with MS-70 being the highest, indicating a perfect coin.

4.1.3 Factors Affecting Coin Grading

Several factors influence a coin's grade:

- Wear: The amount of wear on a coin's surfaces, particularly on high points and design elements, significantly impacts its grade.

- Strike: The quality of the coin's strike, including the sharpness of the design details and any imperfections, is considered when grading.

- Surface Preservation: The presence of scratches, nicks, or other surface blemishes affects a coin's grade. Original luster and eye appeal also play a role.

- Color and Toning: The color and toning of a coin can be both desirable and detrimental. Natural toning can enhance a coin's grade, while artificial toning or discoloration may lower it.

- Bag Marks: Coins that were stored in bags or transported in bulk may exhibit bag marks, which can reduce their grade.

4.1.4 Third-Party Grading Services

To provide an impartial and standardized assessment of coin grades, third-party grading services exist. These organizations, such as the Numismatic Guaranty Corporation (NGC) and the Professional Coin Grading Service (PCGS), employ expert graders who evaluate coins according to established grading criteria. Coins are then encapsulated in tamper-evident holders with a label displaying their grade and other relevant information.

Third-party grading services offer several advantages:

- Authentication: They verify the authenticity of coins, helping to prevent the sale of counterfeit or altered pieces.

- Standardization: Grading services provide consistency and standardization in grading, ensuring that collectors receive an accurate grade for their coins.

- Market Acceptance: Coins graded by reputable services are widely accepted in the numismatic market, making them more attractive to buyers and sellers.

- Protection: Encapsulation protects coins from damage and environmental factors, preserving their condition.

Understanding coin grading is an essential skill for any serious collector. It enables you to assess the condition and value of your coins accurately. Whether you use third-party grading services or learn to grade coins yourself, this knowledge is a valuable tool in your numismatic journey, allowing you to make informed decisions and appreciate the beauty and historical significance of each coin in your collection.

4.2 Determining Coin Value

Determining the value of a coin involves assessing various factors that influence its worth in the numismatic market. While coin grading, as discussed in the previous section, is a significant component of value determination, several other key elements come into play when gauging the monetary value of a coin. In this section, we will explore these factors and how they contribute to determining the value of a coin.

4.2.1 Rarity and Scarcity

Rarity is a primary factor in determining a coin's value. Coins that are rare or scarce tend to command higher prices because they are in limited supply. Factors that influence rarity include:

- Mintage: The number of coins originally produced. Low-mintage coins are often rarer and more valuable.

- Survival Rate: The percentage of coins that have survived over time. Coins that have been well-preserved are scarcer.

- Historical Significance: Coins associated with historical events, figures, or periods can be highly sought after and, therefore, valuable.

4.2.2 Demand and Popularity

The demand for a particular coin can significantly impact its value. Coins that are popular among collectors or have a dedicated following may command higher prices. Demand can be influenced by factors such as:

- Collector Interest: The level of interest from collectors in a specific coin series, design, or historical era.

- Trends: Current trends and market sentiment can drive demand for certain coins. Pop culture, movies, or historical anniversaries can spark increased interest.

- Design and Aesthetics: Coins with appealing designs, artwork, or unique features may attract more collectors.

4.2.3 Condition and Grading

As discussed in Section 4.1, the condition of a coin, as determined by grading, plays a vital role in its value. Coins in higher grades generally command higher prices due to their better overall condition and visual appeal.

4.2.4 Historical Significance

Coins with historical significance, such as those minted during pivotal moments in history or featuring iconic figures, can hold added value. Collectors often seek coins that tell a compelling historical story.

4.2.5 Numismatic Market Trends

The numismatic market is dynamic and can be influenced by trends, economic conditions, and investor interest. Keeping an eye on market trends and staying informed about the current state of the coin market can help collectors make informed decisions about buying and selling.

4.2.6 Market Comparables

Comparing a coin to similar coins that have recently sold in the market can provide a benchmark for its value. Auction results, dealer listings, and sales data from reputable sources can help collectors gauge the current market value of their coins.

4.2.7 Authentication and Certification

Coins that have been authenticated and certified by reputable third-party grading services may have added value due to the assurance of authenticity and accurate grading. Buyers often have more confidence in such coins.

4.2.8 Marketability

A coin's marketability refers to how easily it can be bought or sold. Coins with high marketability are typically more liquid and easier to trade, while coins with limited marketability may take longer to find a buyer.

Determining the value of a coin is a multifaceted process that requires a combination of knowledge, research, and consideration of various factors. It's important to approach value determination with a comprehensive understanding of the coin's attributes and its place in the broader numismatic market. Whether you're assessing the value of a single coin or evaluating an entire collection, the ability to accurately gauge a coin's worth is a valuable skill for any coin collector.

Chapter 5: Building and Organizing Your Collection

Introduction

Having embarked on your numismatic journey and gained insights into the intricacies of coin collecting, you've likely amassed a collection of coins that holds both sentimental and monetary value. In Chapter 5, we delve into the art of building and organizing your coin collection, transforming it from a mere assortment of coins into a meticulously curated and well-preserved treasure trove.

Building a coin collection is not just about acquiring coins haphazardly; it's a deliberate and passionate pursuit. It involves making choices, setting goals, and appreciating the historical and artistic significance of each coin. In this chapter, we explore the strategies and principles that will guide you in building a collection that reflects your interests, values, and aspirations as a collector.

Once you've started building your collection, the next challenge is organization. A well-organized collection allows you to enjoy your coins to the fullest, facilitates research and study, and ensures that your valuable numismatic assets are safeguarded for future generations.

We will cover a range of topics, including setting collecting goals, budgeting, acquiring coins strategically, and selecting the right storage and display methods. Whether you're a novice collector or a seasoned numismatist, this chapter will equip you with the knowledge and tools needed to cultivate and manage your coin collection with care and enthusiasm.

Remember that coin collecting is not just a hobby; it's a journey of discovery, learning, and appreciation. Your collection is a testament to your passion for history, art, and culture, and it will continue to evolve and grow as you explore the fascinating world of numismatics. So, let's embark on this chapter and unlock the secrets to building and organizing a collection that will bring joy and fulfillment to your numismatic adventure.

5.1 Cataloging Your Coins

Cataloging your coins is an essential step in building and organizing your coin collection. Creating a comprehensive catalog allows you to keep track of the coins you own, record important details, and maintain a clear and organized record of your numismatic treasures. In this section, we will explore the significance of coin cataloging and provide guidance on how to effectively catalog your coins.

5.1.1 Why Catalog Your Coins

Cataloging your coins offers several important benefits:

1. Organization: A well-maintained catalog keeps your collection organized and accessible. You can quickly locate specific coins, track your progress, and identify gaps in your collection.

2. Documentation: Catalogs serve as valuable documentation of your collection's history and provenance. They provide a record of when and where you acquired each coin, as well as any pertinent details.

3. Asset Management: Catalogs help you assess the value of your collection for insurance purposes or estate planning. They ensure that you have a clear record of your numismatic assets.

4. Research and Study: A catalog becomes a valuable resource for research and study. It allows you to cross-reference coins, conduct historical research, and explore the nuances of each piece.

5.1.2 Elements of a Coin Catalog

A well-structured coin catalog typically includes the following elements for each coin in your collection:

1. Coin Details: Record the coin's key details, including its denomination, country of origin, mint mark (if applicable), and the year it was minted.

2. Date: Specify the date of acquisition or the date the coin was minted.

3. Grade: Include the coin's grade based on the grading scale discussed in Chapter 4.

4. Value: Document the estimated market value of the coin, either at the time of acquisition or based on current market conditions.

5. Description: Provide a detailed description of the coin's design, features, and any notable characteristics.

6. Acquisition Details: Note how and where you acquired the coin, including the purchase price, seller, or any relevant circumstances.

7. Provenance: Record any known information about the coin's ownership history or previous collections it may have been part of.

8. Special Notes: Use this section for any special notes, anecdotes, or historical information related to the coin.

5.1.3 Methods of Cataloging

There are various methods and tools you can use to catalog your coins:

1. Manual Catalog: Create a physical catalog using notebooks, index cards, or specialized coin cataloging books. This method allows for a hands-on approach to cataloging.

2. Digital Catalog: Use spreadsheet software or numismatic cataloging software to create a digital catalog. Digital catalogs offer flexibility, easy searching, and the ability to include images of your coins.

3. Mobile Apps: There are mobile apps designed specifically for coin collectors that offer user-friendly interfaces for cataloging and tracking coins on your smartphone or tablet.

5.1.4 Tips for Effective Cataloging

Here are some tips to ensure effective coin cataloging:

- Be consistent in your cataloging approach to maintain uniformity and clarity throughout your catalog.

- Include high-quality images of your coins whenever possible to enhance the catalog's visual appeal and usefulness.

- Regularly update your catalog as you acquire new coins or make changes to your collection.

- Consider keeping both physical and digital copies of your catalog for redundancy and accessibility.

Cataloging your coins may require some initial effort, but the benefits far outweigh the time invested. A well-maintained catalog not only helps you manage and enjoy your collection but also provides a valuable record for future generations of collectors or potential buyers. It is a cornerstone of effective coin collection organization and management.